Springs of Living Water

Springs of Living Water

Bible Studies
on Grace and Transformation

Risk BOOK WCC Publications, Geneva

This publication is also available in French, German, Spanish and Portuguese.

The scripture quotations contained herein are from the New Revised Standard Version Bible (except where otherwise specified), copyright, 1989, by the Division of Christian Education of the National Council of the Churches of Christ in the USA. All rights reserved.

Cover design: Marie Arnaud Snakkers
Cover illustration: the logo of the WCC's ninth assembly, Porto Alegre, Brazil, 2006, on the theme "God, in your grace, transform the world"

ISBN 2-8254-1420-4

© 2005 World Council of Churches
150 route de Ferney, P.O. Box 2100
1211 Geneva 2, Switzerland
Website: http://www.wcc-coe.org
http://www.wcc-assembly
No. 109 in the Risk Book Series

Printed in Switzerland

Table of Contents

Introduction

This book invites you to consider the theme of the ninth assembly of the World Council of Churches (Porto Alegre, Brazil, February 2006), "God, in your grace, transform the world", from a biblical perspective and to relate it to your own life and to the witness of your church.

It has been prepared under the guidance and on behalf of the assembly planning committee by a WCC staff group. Seven chapters contain two Bible texts apiece, a concise interpretation, a prayer, and suggestions for linking the text with your own life and context. The first study comes from Brazil, the country where the assembly will be held, and the last chapter brings the reader back to Latin America with a reflection on grace by Christians from that region. The rationale for the choice of the Bible texts is explained at the end of the book.

Women and men living in very specific and diverse contexts have been asked to provide a personal perspective on the passages from the Bible which were given to them. They have written in their own names, drawing on their personal or church experiences, as persons rooted in their spiritual and denominational traditions. The editors have not attempted to unify the various approaches or theological positions. It is of the essence of the ecumenical movement to offer a space for sharing the richness and challenge of a diversity of approaches to and interpretations of the Bible. Suggestions on how to work with the texts have been prepared by Simon Oxley of the WCC staff.

By reading the Bible in common, listening to each other and praying together, Christians from different denominations and all parts of the world are spiritually edified as they progress on their common journey towards the full and visible manifestation of God-given unity.

How to use this book

You can use these Bible studies for personal reflection, but we strongly encourage you to join with others in discussion groups in the time before the assembly. For those who will be attending the assembly, this will be a collaborative way of preparing yourself so that you may arrive already enriched by the insights of others. For those who will be accompanying the assembly at a distance, this study process will help you prepare to be with the participants in spirit.

Working in a group requires careful preparation. At least one member should be thoroughly familiar with the material in order to guide the group. The discussion guide presumes that everyone has read the Bible passages and the reflection. There should be a welcoming and relaxed atmosphere. Sitting in a circle helps interaction. The first part of the process encourages you to begin with your own context and then broaden the conversation. Allow time for people to speak from their experience, but be aware that this may be painful for some. Remember that listening is as important as speaking and that violent words can be just as destructive as physical violence. Build prayer into your time together. Use the prayers written for each Bible study, and add your own prayers. Continue to pray for God's transforming power to be at work in the assembly.

Each of the seven Bible studies ends with a question: How does this Bible study help us understand and respond to the assembly theme "God, in your grace, transform the world"? Collect your answers and use them locally to challenge your congregation or parish, your denomination and council of churches to take action with you in accompanying and building on the foundation of the assembly.

Hand in Hand – So That We May Have Days of Grace

Milton Schwantes and Elaine Neuenfeldt

Luke 4:16-30

When he came to Nazareth, where he had been brought up, he went to the synagogue on the sabbath day, as was his custom. He stood up to read, and the scroll of the prophet Isaiah was given to him. He unrolled the scroll and found the place where it was written: "The Spirit of the Lord is upon me, because he has anointed me to bring good news to the poor. He has sent me to proclaim release to the captives and recovery of sight to the blind, to let the oppressed go free, to proclaim <u>the year of the Lord's favour.</u>" And he rolled up the scroll, gave it back to the attendant, and sat down. The eyes of all in the synagogue were fixed on him. Then he began to say to them, "Today this scripture has been fulfilled in your hearing." All spoke well of him and were amazed at the gracious words that came from his mouth. They said, "Is not this Joseph's son?" He said to them, "Doubtless you will quote to me this proverb, 'Doctor, cure yourself!' And you will say, 'Do here also in your hometown the things that we have heard you did at Capernaum.'" And he said, "Truly I tell you, no prophet is accepted in the prophet's hometown. But the truth is, there were many widows in Israel in the time of Elijah, when the heaven was shut up three years and six months, and there was a severe famine over all the land; yet Elijah was sent to none of them except to a widow at Zarephath in Sidon. There were also many lepers in Israel in the time of the prophet Elisha, and none of them was cleansed except Naaman the Syrian." When they heard this, all in the synagogue were filled with rage. They got up, drove him out of the town, and led him to the brow of the hill on which their town was built, so that they might hurl him off the cliff. But he passed through the midst of them and went on his way.

The authors are both Lutheran pastors with a PhD in biblical science. Prof. Milton Schwantes teaches at the Methodist University of São Paulo in Brazil, and is the coordinator of the periodical RIBLA (Revista de Interpretação Bíblica Latino-Americana), the review of Latin American interpretation of the Bible. Prof. Elaine Neuenfeldt is the co-director of the CEBI (Centro de Estudos Bíblicos), the Brazilian centre for biblical studies. She holds the chair of feminist theology at the theological faculty in São Leopoldo, Brazil. This text has been translated from the original Portuguese by the WCC language service.

> *Isaiah 61:1-4*
> The spirit of the Lord God is upon me, because the Lord has anointed me; he has sent me to bring good news to the oppressed, to bind up the broken-hearted, to proclaim liberty to the captives, and release to the prisoners; to proclaim the year of the Lord's favour, and the day of vengeance of our God; to comfort all who mourn; to provide for those who mourn in Zion – to give them a garland instead of ashes, the oil of gladness instead of mourning, the mantle of praise instead of a faint spirit. They will be called oaks of righteousness, the planting of the Lord, to display his glory. They shall build up the ancient ruins, they shall raise up the former devastations; they shall repair the ruined cities, the devastations of many generations.

The suggestion that we should study the whole passage, Luke 4:16-30, is significant. After all, Jesus' reading of the words of Isaiah and his explanation and application of the text led to his being rejected. His commitment to all the poor, irrespective of origin, made the people who were listening want to kill him. The same feeling of death also pervades Isaiah 61. In the exile, or probably after it, there was extreme poverty. There was no longer anything in people's purses with holes in them, as Haggai expressed it (Hag. 1:6). Verses 1 and 2 of Isaiah 61 are repeated in Luke. But after verse 2, Isaiah 61 continues on its own course: Zion is exalted, with the presence of the Lord God in the midst of the people and community. We need to pay attention to the whole of Isaiah 61 and thus become more aware of the privileged position of the poor and the weak in this "year of the Lord's favour".

That is what it is also like here in Brazil! That is what people here say today when they listen to passages like these from Isaiah and Luke. They are not alien to us. These things are happening here and speak to our experience. They were happening in the time of Isaiah 61 and, some five centuries later, in the time of Jesus. And equally, they are happening today in our world. That is how the Bible comes across to us. In recent decades we have been discovering it on our own soil, in our lives and hopes. We feel ourselves to be much closer to that world of the Bible than to the great shopping centres which, beautiful though they are, are not our real world. The struggles in the Bible are much closer to our own. The Bible is a present contemporary reality in the hearts, eyes and feet of people here – women, children and men. It is a gracious gift of God to us that we can actually experience this in our own land. The Bible is among us.

As we go about our daily lives, in this world of people without hope, these narratives can be seen in living forms in people's bodies. As we listen to people with nothing to call their own, we are hearing the holy words of God. As we live in our communities, we are living by God's grace. Indeed, the Bible comes alive for us by way of these people who are suffering and hoping for better days. People in poverty are calling us in the churches to wake up as we travel on the road from Jericho to Jerusalem (cf. Luke 10:25-37 and Acts 2-6). A link has been made between the Bible and those who suffer. We cling to that.

Sheer observation would not enable us to speak like this. We can say it because we are empowered by the Spirit. Ultimately, it is the Spirit who guides the course of events in Luke 4:16-30. In the Spirit, Jesus comes to Galilee (Luke 4:14-15) and places himself within the sphere of the Spirit (Luke 4:18-19); and, anointed by the Spirit, he utters striking words. He quotes them in part from Isaiah, but in such a way that they become his guiding stars for a journey. What Jesus makes clear to see was already there – it had already been said by all the prophets – but now it can no longer be ignored. This reinterpretation of Isaiah that Jesus makes is a revival of prophecy, and he applies it to daily life and its challenges. This way of reading scripture inspires us to adopt a method that encourages "popular reading of the Bible", in which you may read the message behind the words and beyond the words. This is a passage that strengthens and affirms the poor in their reading of the Bible. It becomes possible to recover the vitality of the narrative, beginning with the stance taken against the structures that imprison and oppress people.

Access to land, essential for life in dignity

There are five tasks for the Messiah, the anointed one, the last of the five, "proclaiming the year of the Lord's favour" (Luke 4:19) being the decisive and ultimately important one. The year of God's favour is a celebration of the right of all people to a share in social goods, especially land (cf. Lev. 25). A life of dignity entails access to land. If people are landless, they live a dehumanized life. The tragedy of Brazil is that there are millions with nothing, and land is owned by a few. Five hundred years of life without land to call one's own has resulted in wretched *favelas* and impoverished settlements. Oh, that God would grant us a year of favour by opening gates and breaking down fences!

The year of the Lord's favour is the supreme blessing. Four details stand out: two take the form of words and two take the form of acts; in the world of the Bible, word and action are two aspects of the same reality. The poor have the good news preached to them, since in God's grace their misfortune is dispelled. The prisoners will have freedom proclaimed to them. These two prospects vie with each another in the people's ardent desire for a new life. The year of the Lord's favour also manifests itself in recovery of sight for the blind and in release for the oppressed. The year of the Lord's favour is worth striving for because the words describing it are amazing, and its liberating actions are a joy. They all are "gracious words" (Luke 4:22).

With his words favouring the poor and hurting, women and children, Jesus is excluding no one. The problem is that many of us prefer an exclusive space. The more things are the exclusive preserve of some, the less remains for the poor. Jesus founded a church and not an exclusive club for its members.

Prophecy had already declared this. We read it everywhere in the Bible. We pray it in the Psalms. The wisdom literature inculcates it. If there is no place for the widow and the oppressed in the community, it cannot be the people of God. The whole book of Isaiah cries aloud: little children, the widows and the poor are "my people" (cf. 3:15) and "the Servant" is the sign of God's presence (Isa. 42:1-4,52-53). Indeed, hope itself has its roots in those fragile beings, children, who are "signs and symbols in Israel from the Lord" (Isa. 8:16-18; cf. Isa. 7:10-17, 9:1-6, 11:1-5).

This is the context of Isaiah 61 and of prophecy in general. It is the foundation of Jesus' words at Nazareth. Moreover, these prophecies form more than the foundation: they define the structure itself. There is no need to see disagreement between the First and Second Testaments. In both, life is seen so comprehensively that we discover it is faith that nourishes it. The best approach is to open ourselves lovingly to both Old and New Testament teachings so as to bring peoples together. In fact, Luke 4 is permeated with suppositions drawn from the Hebrew scriptures.

Isaiah 61 speaks of a people in the midst of cruelty, of an exile that had become for them all a valley of dry bones (Ezek. 37). They are slaves with bruised, wounded and tortured faces (Isa. 40-55). But it is from this condition that a new people emerges out of ruins and weariness (Isa. 40). It is impossible to read the whole of Isaiah, passing through the experience of exile in Babylon, without linking this body of prophecy with our own history. Sometimes we see it, and at other times we ignore it. In the end, it sometimes becomes more pleasant for modern Brazilians to harken back to our trans-Atlantic origins: to dream of Europe is to seem more sophisticated. Our wounds are too many, and there seems to be no solution. Indigenous and African-Brazilian women are still weeping and lamenting. We frequently feel that Latin America and the Caribbean are not good places. We do have many joys, but there is also weeping in our fields and hovels.

Grace encourages

It is thus our duty to seek refuge in Zion. Verses 1 and 2 of Isaiah 61 are quoted in Luke 4:18-19. But Isaiah 61 in verse 3 goes on to emphasize Zion. And this emphasis helps us to make the vision in Luke 4 a reality, where it might have remained no more than a beautiful and good intention. Luke 4 could have inspired us to a purely individual conviction, without communal reference, without involvement with a group of persons who together can strengthen one another to become "fit to join in the struggle", as we say. When we see the prophet referring to Zion, we see that we need to unite with one another in order to move out from beneath the burden of our suffering. That can happen only if we join hand in hand! This form of power overcomes; the child in the manger unites. If we do not all come together, we shall be thrust into endless misery. That is the difference between "ashes" and "crowns", as expressed in verse 3. If we remain alone, even with the best of intentions, we simply dissipate our efforts. But if, by the grace of God, we become "Zion", "the oil of gladness" will be spread abroad. Our communities must become "oil of gladness" for our lives.

Finally, verses 3 and 4 are a wonderful invitation. If we do not pay attention to them, we shall be missing an extraordinary ecumenical opportunity. After all, some use the Bible itself to create division. They use its words to play people off against one another. The most ancient division is what distinguishes and separates Christians from Jews. It is thus essential for us to pray to God for new ecumenical paths along which the different churches and the different religions can journey together.

Here is the encouragement that grace gives us. The anointed, crowned and liberated bodies will be called "oaks of righteousness", or of justice (Isa. 61:3). This prophecy evokes a vision of a new creation. Once again, the creatures are welcomed and given names (cf. Gen. 2:19). Life is recreated on the foundation of the experience and practice of justice, and on the basis of that justice people are reintegrated into the fabric of society. They are new creatures and are relocated in a garden of justice.

Prayer

God of many names, we pray:

Come to us, come and journey with us,

so that we may walk in your grace and peace.

Fill us with hope, so that we may break through barriers.

Inspire us on our ecumenical journey, making possible encounters and dialogue.

Send your Spirit to strengthen us in our prophetic role of proclaiming liberation.

May your Spirit be a gentle breeze when we need comfort and security.

But let it be a strong wind when we are too settled and need to speak out.

Let your life-giving peace come into our bodies and be expressed in action for peace between people, between churches and religions, and between nations.

May your world-transforming grace inspire us to join hands and declare the freedom given by your love.

Shower your blessings upon us as we journey on, announcing the good news of justice, caring and acceptance. Amen.

MS and EN

How to work with these texts

- After reading Luke 4:16-30 and Isaiah 61:1-4, do you agree with Milton Schwantes and Elaine Neuenfeldt that we may feel closer to the world of those passages than to our "great shopping centres"? Where does your own daily experience relate to this?

- Inspired by the Spirit, Jesus sets out the purpose of his ministry in Luke 4:18-19. How should this guide the ministry of the church with the poor, those in captivity, the blind and the oppressed? What are our churches actually doing to bring good news, release, recovery and freedom? Make a list of specific examples and comment on them.

- Imagine that you are a non-believer with the sounds of natural disaster, of war and the cries of the poor in your ears. Then you hear Christians talking about the "year of the Lord's favour". What might you think? How does our ministry make the proclamation of the "year of the Lord's favour" credible?

- Milton Schwantes and Elaine Neuenfeldt describe Isaiah 61:3-4 as "a wonderful invitation" and talk about the "encouragement that grace gives to us". Tell one another stories of how you experience God working in and through us to bring hope.

- How does this Bible study help us understand and respond to the assembly theme "God, in your grace, transform the world"?

"New Heavens and a New Earth"

Lopeti Taufa

Isaiah 65:17-25

For I am about to create new heavens and a new earth; the former things shall not be remembered or come to mind. But be glad and rejoice forever in what I am creating; for I am about to create Jerusalem as a joy, and its people as a delight. I will rejoice in Jerusalem, and delight in my people; no more shall the sound of weeping be heard in it, or the cry of distress. No more shall there be in it an infant that lives but a few days, or an old person who does not live out a life-time; for one who dies at a hundred years will be considered a youth, and one who falls short of a hundred will be considered accursed. They shall build houses and inhabit them; they shall plant vineyards and eat their fruit. They shall not build and another inhabit; they shall not plant and another eat; for like the days of a tree shall the days of my people be, and my chosen shall long enjoy the work of their hands. They shall not labour in vain, or bear children for calamity; for they shall be offspring blessed by the Lord - and their descendants as well. Before they call I will answer, while they are yet speaking I will hear. The wolf and the lamb shall feed together, the lion shall eat straw like the ox; but the serpent – its food shall be dust! They shall not hurt or destroy on all my holy mountain, says the Lord.

Revelation 21:1-8

Then I saw a new heaven and a new earth; for the first heaven and the first earth had passed away, and the sea was no more. And I saw the holy city, the new Jerusalem, coming down out of heaven from God, prepared as a bride adorned for her husband. And I heard a loud voice from the throne saying, "See, the home of God is among mortals. He will dwell with them; they will be his peoples, and God himself will be with them; he will wipe every tear from their eyes. Death will be no more; mourning and crying and pain will be no more, for the first things have passed away." And the one who was seated on the throne said, "See, I am making all things new." Also

---

Rev. Dr Lopeti Taufa is a former president of the Free Wesleyan Church of Tonga. During his tenure as president, he served on the executive committee of the Pacific Conference of Churches and taught at the Methodist Theological College.

> he said, "Write this, for these words are trustworthy and true." Then he said to me, "It is done! I am the Alpha and the Omega, the beginning and the end. To the thirsty I will give water as a gift from the spring of the water of life. Those who conquer will inherit these things, and I will be their God and they will be my children. But as for the cowardly, the faithless, the polluted, the murderers, the fornicators, the sorcerers, the idolaters, and all liars, their place will be in the lake that burns with fire and sulfur, which is the second death."

The texts of this Bible study are visions of God's creative and transforming power at work, making all things new, now and in the future.

The Isaiah passage is in the form of divine speech which powerfully asserts the transforming power of God in the universe and history. In response to the laments and complaints of the post-exilic community in Israel (Isa. 63:15-64:12), God says:

> "For behold, I create new heavens
> and a new earth:
> and the former things shall not be remembered
> or come to mind.
> But be glad and rejoice forever
> In that which I create;
> for behold, I create in Jerusalem a rejoicing
> and her people a joy."
> (Isa. 65:17-18, RSV)

We need to note, among other significant points:
1. God is active in this divine re-creation of the new heavens and a new earth. Divine creative and transforming activity makes its divine mark in the new age.
2. The use of the participial form of the verb "to create" in the original Hebrew version of the passage pulls the divine creative activity into the present time.
3. The cosmological characteristics of the heavens and the earth have been radically transformed and redeemed.

4. The new Jerusalem comes from above, that is, from God.
5. The former things shall not be remembered; the new age has been ushered in, and the messianic city is characterized by the messianic banquet and joy.
6. An important relationship is established in the new creation, namely, between God and the people of God, the elect. In contrast with universalistic outlooks in other chapters or books of the Bible, it is a change in the nation's relationship with the Lord that transforms the cosmos.

In the new age, the community will be redeemed. Under God a new stage in history is set. Relationships with God will be of such intimacy that God is ready to answer the redeemed even before they call on him (65:24).

The characteristic features of the community in the new age are described broadly in verses 20 and following. People will enjoy the fruits of their own labours (v.21); unusually long life is set before them (v.22). People will build their own dwellings (v.22). The same thing is true for land, people, plant and harvest (v.22). Finally, humans will be fertile, producing their offspring (v.23).

As to the quality of life, the intimacy between God and humans transforms the cosmos itself, overturning the natural order of violence between wolf and lamb, or lion and ox, giving way to peace (v.25).

This powerful vision depicting a utopia needs further scrutiny. One should be mindful of propagating a new utopian doctrine without sounding socially naive or appearing to be an other-worldly escapist. The utopian doctrine can be proclaimed with integrity only in the context of the worshipping community itself.

The optimistic outlook of Isaiah suggests there is hope for the situations and needs of various communities throughout the Pacific today. We are mindful of the political turmoil in countries such as the Solomon Islands, Papua New Guinea and Fiji, the desolate situations of low-lying, resource-poor nations throughout Micronesia and Polynesia, and the corruption among government leaders in many other countries.

Today, the exilic community of the Pacific is comprised of:
1) disillusioned migrants who seek better opportunities for work and study in nearby developed countries;
2) helpless victims left behind by those who leave;
3) the disappointed public who feel robbed of their freedom and rights to a fair and good life;
4) the concerned majority who would like to trust but find no security in trusting their leaders to administer political, social and economic aspects of their life;
5) the marginal believers and youth who are less and less convinced by the healing power of the church;
6) leaders who propagate a "better life" without God.

The modern Pacific exile is a displaced person, both physically and spiritually. Yet the idea of a new heaven and a new earth remains for such a person an ultimately desirable objective. The image suggests that in this re-created cosmos, all will be renewed and an equilibrium of fairness will be achieved. Isaiah prophesies divine intervention. This divinity is the differentiating factor in believers' and non-believers' concepts of a transformed society — yet it is only in this divinity that transformation is possible.

Our call for God's transforming power is our admission that only God can make a difference. Without God, there is no difference, for it is God alone who creates and re-creates. The spiritual shift of Pacific people caught in the waves of distrust, disillusionment, hopelessness, alcoholism and other social predicaments has caused a widening chasm which must be filled by a call to intimacy with God. This intimacy is found in the creation of peace, trust and hope and the return from exile to a greater and deeper relationship with God. Christians are called to make God's presence better known in various aspects of life, by becoming themselves (ourselves!) the vessels through which God's character is made known.

As the laments and complaints of Israel were heard by God, and as the prophet relayed their coming liberation, we now are called to respond to the laments and complaints of Pacific peoples in this contemporary era. We are called to relay the message that God's kingdom is at hand, and that this kingdom, which consists of God's peace and love, is achievable. God's transforming power is not just physical power but also a spiritual strength through which lives are bettered and integrity is refined. All this may be achieved only through God's transforming power.

LT

Prayer

Creating and re-creating God,
Our hope is in you.
        Hear our cries and laments.
Bless our vision for
transformed relations,
sustainable communities,
a pacific, peace-loving world.

Holy God, creative power,
our strength is in you.
We long for you.
Guide us, inspire us,
as we join in the dance of life.

In your grace, and in the mission of our Lord Jesus Christ,
abundant life is offered and is possible.
In your transforming grace and power
we become a people of joy.
In the name of the triune God, the Father, Son
        and the Holy Spirit, we pray. Amen.

Elizabeth S. Tapia, 2005

How to work with these texts

- Lopeti Taufa describes what is happening to people in the Pacific. If you were writing this reflection from your own context, what would you say about the people of your nation or region? Writing it down may help you think about it. Do you find the same relevance in the messages of Isaiah 65 and Revelation 21 as you hear the promise of a new heaven and a new earth?

- Look at the characteristic features of the new age described in the two passages. Make a list of them, and then think about them one by one. What do each of these say about the quality of life in the promised community? Where do we see each already present in the life of our churches and communities, even in a small way? Do these passages simply offer a better life in the future, or do they challenge us to begin to realize them now? What actions would we have to take for our churches to become living examples of the new community?

- How does this Bible study help us understand and respond to the assembly theme "God, in your grace, transform the world"?

God Shows No Partiality

Susan Durber

Jonah 4:1-11

But this was very displeasing to Jonah, and he became angry. He prayed to the Lord and said, "O Lord! Is not this what I said while I was still in my own country? That is why I fled to Tarshish at the beginning; for I knew that you are a gracious God and merciful, slow to anger, and abounding in steadfast love, and ready to relent from punishing. And now, O Lord, please take my life from me, for it is better for me to die than to live." And the Lord said, "Is it right for you to be angry?"

Then Jonah went out of the city and sat down east of the city, and made a booth for himself there. He sat under it in the shade, waiting to see what would become of the city. The Lord God appointed a bush, and made it come up over Jonah, to give shade over his head, to save him from his discomfort; so Jonah was very happy about the bush. But when dawn came up the next day, God appointed a worm that attacked the bush, so that it withered. When the sun rose, God prepared a sultry east wind, and the sun beat down on the head of Jonah so that he was faint and asked that he might die. He said, "It is better for me to die than to live." But God said to Jonah, "Is it right for you to be angry about the bush?" And he said, "Yes, angry enough to die." Then the Lord said, "You are concerned about the bush, for which you did not labour and which you did not grow; it came into being in a night and perished in a night. And should I not be concerned about Nineveh, that great city, in which there are more than a hundred and twenty thousand persons who do not know their right hand from their left, and also many animals?"

Acts 10:9-35

About noon the next day, as they were on their journey and approaching the city, Peter went up on the roof to pray. He became hungry and wanted something to eat; and while it was being prepared, he fell into a trance. He saw the heaven opened and something like a large sheet coming

---

Rev. Dr Susan Durber is a minister of the United Reformed Church in the United Kingdom and serves two congregations in Oxford, England. She has a doctorate in biblical studies and literary theory and has published sermons, prayers and articles.

down, being lowered to the ground by its four corners. In it were all kinds of four-footed creatures and reptiles and birds of the air. Then he heard a voice saying, "Get up, Peter; kill and eat." But Peter said, "By no means, Lord; for I have never eaten anything that is profane or unclean." The voice said to him again, a second time, "What God has made clean, you must not call profane." This happened three times, and the thing was suddenly taken up to heaven. Now while Peter was greatly puzzled about what to make of the vision that he had seen, suddenly the men sent by Cornelius appeared. They were asking for Simon's house and were standing by the gate. They called out to ask whether Simon, who was called Peter, was staying there.

While Peter was still thinking about the vision, the Spirit said to him, "Look, three men are searching for you. Now get up, go down, and go with them without hesitation; for I have sent them." So Peter went down to the men and said, "I am the one you are looking for; what is the reason for your coming?" They answered, "Cornelius, a centurion, an upright and God-fearing man, who is well spoken of by the whole Jewish nation, was directed by a holy angel to send for you to come to his house and to hear what you have to say." So Peter invited them in and gave them lodging.

The next day he got up and went with them, and some of the believers from Joppa accompanied him. The following day they came to Caesarea. Cornelius was expecting them and had called together his relatives and close friends. On Peter's arrival Cornelius met him and, falling at his feet, worshipped him. But Peter made him get up, saying, "Stand up; I am only a mortal." And as he talked with him, he went in and found that many had assembled; and he said to them, "You yourselves know that it is unlawful for a Jew to associate with or to visit a Gentile; but God has shown me that I should not call anyone profane or unclean. So when I was sent for, I came without objection. Now may I ask why you sent for me?" Cornelius replied, "Four days ago at this very hour, at three o'clock, I was praying in my house when suddenly a man in dazzling clothes stood before me. He said, 'Cornelius, your prayer has been heard and your alms have been remembered before God. Send therefore to Joppa and ask for Simon, who is called Peter; he is staying in the home of Simon, a tanner, by the sea.' Therefore I sent for you immediately, and you have been kind enough to come. So now all of us are here in the presence of God to listen to all that the Lord has commanded you to say."

> Then Peter began to speak to them: "I truly understand that God shows no partiality, but in every nation anyone who fears him and does what is right is acceptable to him."

For much of the time we pretend that we are predominantly rational creatures and that reasoned argument is the best way to change our minds. The American Declaration of Independence proclaims that certain truths are "self-evident" (to reason) and most of us, generally, agree. But we also know that we are not solely creatures of reason. We are prey to irrational fears, subject to ancient taboos, held bound by forces we scarcely understand. To bring about a change of heart sometimes requires more than an appeal to reason.

God chooses some astonishing ways to change our minds and hearts. These seem rarely to involve an academic paper and some neatly argued logic. The story of Jonah provides a good example of God's powerful gifts of persuasion. In offering an explanation of why God had forgiven the Ninevites, God does not present Jonah with a long and carefully worded case. Instead, with a gentle and persuasive trick, God uses a castor oil plant and the midday sun. If Jonah can protest at the shrivelling of a pot plant, God says, "Should I not be concerned about Nineveh, that great city, in which there are more than a hundred and twenty thousand persons who do not know their right hand from their left?"

It's hard to know whether Jonah was ever completely convinced. But the narrator of the whole story of Jonah evidently hopes that the reader will be convinced that God cares about all the people in creation, even those the reader has been taught to reckon foreign, immoral and undeserving. The story is part of the prophetic witness of our faith tradition that "God shows no partiality", or perhaps, more truthfully still, that God loves all of us like favourites.

In convincing the apostle Peter of the same truth, God also does something more than present the argument. In any case, as we think about what "the argument" might be, we can at least conclude that the modern human-rights agenda or the post-Enlightenment understanding of the equality of all human beings would have been lost on a first-century apostle. It's striking, of course, that this argument is lost even on many who live today, centuries "post-" all of that. The forces that keep notions of racial separation or ethnic superiority going are always rooted in places other than reason. And so it was into those places that God made a move, and changed Peter's understanding.

You can feel sorry for Peter. He had been praying hard up there on the roof, and in the heat of the day. He became hungry, in fact so hungry that he fell into a trance while the meal was still cooking. And like a starved man he dreamt of food. But this was a nightmare. He was being invited to eat anything, including food that he had learned to find disgusting and abhorrent. It wasn't just that it was off the menu or against the rules; it was the kind of offer that made even a hungry man feel nauseous. But the voice inviting him to eat said clearly, three times, "What God has made clean, you must not call profane." Peter is frankly puzzled about what the nightmare could mean, until he is taken to meet a Gentile. And then Peter recognizes a link between his dream-induced nausea and the disgust and distaste he has, up to that point, felt for the Gentiles. If God could so radically challenge all that Peter had learned at a gut level about food, how much more could God challenge what Peter had learned at this deep, irrational level about human beings.

Peter says, "God has shown me that I should not call anyone profane or unclean."

It is a mark of human maturity to recognize that many of our deepest feelings about other people are rooted somewhere that may not be open to the straightforward claims of reason. We know, at the level of our minds, that it is unreasonable to believe that God prefers some people to others or that some ethnic groups are superior to others. But sometimes, in a place within ourselves which we can hardly name, feelings of fear or even of disgust emerge. It is into this place that we need God to come and show us the truth, as God revealed it to Peter in his famished dream of a tablecloth laden with taboo food.

In Amitav Ghosh's post-colonial novel, *The Glass Palace*, the author describes how the British colonialists tried to force the members of the Indian army, under their rule, to break their various food taboos, so that they would forget their differences from one another and forge a new loyalty to the British empire.

Every meal at an officers' mess... was an adventure, a glorious infringement of taboos. They ate foods that none of them had ever touched at home: bacon, ham and sausages at breakfast; roast beef and pork chops for dinner... All of them had stories to tell about how their stomachs had turned the first time they had chewed upon a piece of beef or pork; they had struggled to keep the morsels down, fighting their revulsion.[1]

This story illustrates a connection between food taboos and the tragedy of racial separation as well as conveying something of the real cost of a broken taboo. It is also a scandalous story to us who read of it now because of the political context from which it comes. The British attempted to overcome one kind of separation, but only for their own imperial ends *and* in order to reinforce yet another kind of colonial oppression. But, from whatever place we read this scandalous text, it may stir and invoke within us a renewed sense of the "scandal" of the breaking of food laws and taboos. And to do that is to renew our sense of what it was that Peter faced in his dream.

It is a taken-for-granted foundation of the church in our times that racism is a sin and that God has no favourites. In Christ we are brothers and sisters, no matter where we come from, of whatever nation or tribe. This has, tragically, not always been so. But it may be that we are still reluctant to face the fear of the other that is rooted in a deep place, and a place which cannot always be reached by the powers of argument or reason. Occasionally we catch ourselves out, and the fear of the other or the unknown re-emerges. Perhaps we are at ease in the street if followed by someone who looks like us, but uneasy if we turn to see a face that is foreign to us. Perhaps there are some peoples we cannot dissociate from a history or politics that is fearful to us. Like the smell of foreign food, we are sometimes intrigued and sometimes wary. If this is indeed true about us, then it is better to say it than to pretend. And, more than that, it is good to read in the Bible about the saints and prophets who have struggled to overcome a deeply rooted fear or taboo, and whom God has changed.

Peter's dream changed his mind and changed his heart, so that he was convinced at last that "God shows no partiality". As he preached, the Holy Spirit came upon the Gentiles. And what could Peter do, but recommend that they be baptized? The truth was also pressed upon Jonah that God loves all the people God has made. Both of these texts speak of defining moments in the awakening of particular communities to the end of racial exclusivism – and, in their particular cases, to a new understanding of the relationship between Jews and Gentiles. For, in the sight of God, it turns out, no one is profane or unclean.

Prayer

God of all nations and peoples,

for whom no one on earth is unclean, untouchable or taboo,

cleanse our hearts from the fears and prejudices

which still threaten our being

and challenge us in the deepest places

of body and spirit.

Come to us, and do whatever it takes,

to open our eyes,

to bring a change of heart,

and to turn us to do what is right,

so that, in your good time,

we shall recognize one another

as beloved brothers and sisters,

and as children of your love.

In the name of the one who

broke taboos,

to touch, to heal and to hold,

Jesus Christ your Son, our Saviour,

Amen.

SD

Note:

1. London, Harper Collins, 2000, p.278.

How to work with these texts

• When was the last time you changed your mind? It might, for example, have been about how you valued another person, the desirability of an action or the correctness of a belief. What caused you to change in this way? Spend time thinking about this. It took some dramatic events to change Jonah's and Peter's preconceptions. What parts of these two accounts do you most identify with?

• Jonah and Peter had some deep-seated problems with certain people, which they expressed in relation to their own faith in God. They were certain of the rightness of their positions. Which people do you have problems with? What is it about them that causes the problem – for instance, their ethnicity, their behaviour, their politics or their beliefs? What is it about you that causes the problem – for instance, your personal or communal history, your beliefs, a gut reaction? Be as honest as possible in looking at yourself. If you are discussing this in a group, identify any common factors in your attitudes.

- Susan Durber comments that the narrator of Jonah "hopes that the reader will be convinced that God cares about all the people in creation, even those the reader has been taught to reckon foreign, immoral and undeserving". However, even when we "know" this, we still find it difficult to accept one another. How can God help us change our attitudes and behaviour towards others?

- How does this Bible study help us understand and respond to the assembly theme "God, in your grace, transform the world"?

The World of Untouchables in India

Vedanayagam Devasahayam

Mark 10:32-45

They were on the road, going up to Jerusalem, and Jesus was walking ahead of them; they were amazed, and those who followed were afraid. He took the twelve aside again and began to tell them what was to happen to him, saying, "See, we are going up to Jerusalem, and the Son of Man will be handed over to the chief priests and the scribes, and they will condemn him to death; then they will hand him over to the Gentiles; they will mock him, and spit upon him, and flog him, and kill him; and after three days he will rise again." James and John, the sons of Zebedee, came forward to him and said to him, "Teacher, we want you to do for us whatever we ask of you." And he said to them, "What is it you want me to do for you?" And they said to him, "Grant us to sit, one at your right hand and one at your left, in your glory." But Jesus said to them, "You do not know what you are asking. Are you able to drink the cup that I drink, or be baptized with the baptism that I am baptized with?" They replied, "We are able." Then Jesus said to them, "The cup that I drink you will drink; and with the baptism with which I am baptized, you will be baptized; but to sit at my right hand or at my left is not mine to grant, but it is for those for whom it has been prepared." When the ten heard this, they began to be angry with James and John. So Jesus called them and said to them, "You know that among the Gentiles those whom they recognize as their rulers lord it over them, and their great ones are tyrants over them. But it is not so among you; but whoever wishes to become great among you must be your servant, and whoever wishes to be first among you must be slave of all. For the Son of Man came not to be served but to serve, and to give his life a ransom for many."

Philippians 2:1-11

If then there is any encouragement in Christ, any consolation from love, any sharing in the Spirit, any compassion and sympathy, make my joy complete: be of the same mind, having the same love, being in full accord and of

Bishop Vedanayagam Devasahayam is involved in theological reflection from the context of the Dalits (untouchables) in India. For more than a decade he has been specializing in reading the Bible from the perspective of the marginalized, including Dalits and women. At present he serves the Church of South India as the bishop in the diocese of Madras.

one mind. Do nothing from selfish ambition or conceit, but in humility regard others as better than yourselves. Let each of you look not to your own interests, but to the interests of others. Let the same mind be in you that was in Christ Jesus, who, though he was in the form of God, did not regard equality with God as something to be exploited, but emptied himself, taking the form of a slave, being born in human likeness. And being found in human form, he humbled himself and became obedient to the point of death – even death on a cross. Therefore God also highly exalted him and gave him the name that is above every name, so that at the name of Jesus every knee should bend, in heaven and on earth and under the earth, and every tongue should confess that Jesus Christ is Lord, to the glory of God the Father.

But a Sudra, whether bought or unbought, he may be compelled to do servile work; for he was created by the Self-existent to be the slave of a Brahmin.
A Sudra, though emancipated by his master, is not released from servitude; since that is innate in him, who can set him free from it? [1]

The Dalits, the untouchables of India, who number over 250 million, are the victims of the Hindu caste system – an oppressive social hierarchy built on the principles of ritual purity and pollution, segregation and social exclusion.

The dominant religious, political and social powers have assigned the lowest place in the social ladder to the Dalits to be the slaves and servants of their upper-caste masters. They live in segregated dwellings outside the village and are a despised and excluded people. Humiliation, mockery, contempt, depravation, rape, torture and at times cruel deaths are the treatment they receive from the non-Dalits. Though they are poor and often betrayed by upper-caste people, they are a serving people, habitually depriving themselves and making others rich.

Dalits constitute a vast majority of the Indian church. They have experienced God's grace in Jesus Christ and have been transformed "from no people to God's people" (1 Pet. 2:10). Yet to their great dismay, they continue to experience caste discrimination even within the churches. Through their failure both to comprehend the cen-

tral gospel affirmation (Gal. 3:28) and to develop a life-style different from the oppressive caste culture (Matt. 5:13-16), the churches
have betrayed the faith that has brought them into being.

The text: transformation through God's grace

The text focuses on the disciples, on Jesus and on their relationship with one another.

The disciples: This account, though embarrassing to the apostles,
witnesses to the authenticity of the gospel narratives. Mark's
description of the attitudes of the disciples reminds us of the Indian
situation where the non-Dalits oppress the Dalits.

The disciples are presented as selfish, ambitious and jealous.
They were aspiring for places of honour, seeking to guarantee for
themselves higher status and proximity to glory and power. India's
caste edifice was built in order to award all these favours to the
upper-caste people.

James and John wanted to be rewarded with a higher status
because of the close family relationship and their mother's service to
Jesus. Other disciples were also aspiring for higher positions because
of their closeness to Jesus. Their aspirations also reflected their selfish ambitions. In India, the Brahmins who are the custodians of
orthodox Hinduism have legislated for themselves many rights and
privileges. Through the doctrine of karma, Brahminical Hinduism
encourages social irresponsibility, as it holds each individual respon-
sible for one's predicament.

In the narrative of Mark 10, we find the disciples unable to grasp
or understand the essence of Jesus' teaching. They have misunder-
stood their calling and have not discerned the cost of discipleship.
They seemed to think that closeness to Jesus will result in higher
status, power and authority instead of danger, suffering, shame and
humiliation.

Jesus as one in solidarity with the excluded: In spite of the immi-
nent threat to his life, Jesus differed radically from his disciples. He
exhibited courage and impatience to fulfil his mission. He submitted
himself to God's purposes and turned to God as his only source of
strength. Jesus obeyed and acknowledged God as the ultimate

bestower of honour and glory. Dalits as a serving people have always understood their service to humanity as a service of God.

Jesus found himself utterly lonely despite his physical proximity to the disciples. They seemed to understand his vision and strategy on a completely different level. Selfish ambitions, rivalry and enmity alienate people from one another, especially the disempowered and the excluded. The Dalits suffer just such loneliness due to the hostility of the non-Dalits.

By refusing to comply with the request made by his disciples and by opting for a vocation of service and sacrifice, Jesus identified with humanity in all our frailty and weaknesses. The text from the epistle to the Philippians tells us that he "emptied" himself. Like the untouchables he encountered rejection, mockery, contempt, suffering and violent death. The dominant religious and political structures put him through all this. This has been the exact experience of the Dalits. The word "Dalit" literally means broken, torn, crushed, rent asunder. Thus the cross may serve as the appropriate symbol of Dalitness.

The relationship between Jesus and the disciples: Graciousness characterizes Jesus' response to his disciples, and that transforms them.

Jesus did not consider the request of James and John as presumptuous but taught them patiently what it means to demand to be close to him in glory. By casting himself in the role and vocation of a servant, he made it clear that as one moves farther in discipleship, one is to expect more danger and more suffering. Despite this admonition, the disciples continued to follow Jesus. Their relationship to the master, though imperfect, did not break when their aspirations were denied.

Jesus however responded to James and John by telling them, "The cup that I drink you will drink", a prophecy which came true. James was the first martyr among the apostles, and John suffered over a long period of time for the sake of the gospel. The failures of the disciples during Jesus' life-time were not the final word about their faithfulness. The foolish, lowly, inferior and powerless disciples were transformed by God's grace into holy, powerful, courageous and saintly apostles.

The emergent gospel: a new community in Christ: The implications of the gospel of Jesus Christ emerge at the interface between the context and the text, giving rise to a new community in Christ. Jesus identified certain important features of this new community.

First comes the dynamic of self-renunciation. The epistle text (Phil. 2:5-7) affirms that Jesus, who was in the form of God, did not cling to his equality with God but emptied himself. Jesus did not use his equality with God for his own advantage. He did not claim for himself status and honour. He willingly subjected himself to a life of service and sacrifice. It is through such self-emptying that Jesus revealed who God is, by taking the form of a slave, one who willingly serves and offers his life for the other. Many of those who have worked with the Dalit communities in India have affirmed their faith in this way. In the face of Jesus we see the face of the Dalit, and in the face of the Dalit we see the face of Jesus.

Jesus presents a radical differentiation between God's economy and the world's economy. He holds that power is not a privilege or an instrument of oppression but a responsibility; its exercise is an act of affirming and sustaining life. The Gentiles who give the illusion of exercising the right to rule simply exploit people. Jesus said: "This is not so among you" (Mark 10:43). He envisioned this radical differentiation through the eradication of rank and precedence among disciples and the rejection of power and status in the new community. This makes the Jesus community a counter-cultural community, perhaps one with a permanent minority status.

Jesus emphasized the importance and centrality of service in the new community. Jesus held serving, expending oneself for the other, as a divine virtue. By making himself a slave, he put himself totally at the disposal of others.

He was aware that the purpose of his suffering and death was to be understood as a "ransom". Ransom is the money paid to buy the freedom of those under bondage such as slaves, prisoners of war, condemned criminals and those who have been kidnapped. As a ransom, Jesus has transformed an empty curse into a blessing and a perception of nothingness into a conviction of abundance. For Jesus, serving is in fact saving or liberating people from bondage.

Jesus is a ransom for the liberation of Dalits living in the shackles of the caste system, and this ransom provides hope for a new future.

Because Jesus emptied himself, God has exalted him (Phil. 2:9), made him sit at the right hand of God the Father. The ascended Lord is not resting but is involved in a struggle to put down all his enemies under his foot. The exalted Lord inspires us in our struggle.

Christians are not to compromise with evils that alienate and exclude others, such as casteism, racism, sexism, etc. It will be a poor state of affairs if our witness through our lives and relationships is in no way better than the witnesses given by those who practise and perpetrate these demonic structures and cultures.

The test of adequacy of service or of a servant leader is this: Do those who are served grow as persons, become wiser, just, and more likely themselves to become servants? Jesus' disciples became better people in every conceivable way after they met him and committed themselves as servants for the transformation of the world. The effectiveness of churches' programmes of liberation and justice should be assessed on the basis of resultant transformation among the Dalits.

The humiliation and crucifixion of Jesus was a degrading and cruel event. Those who were crucified were labelled as God-forsaken or cursed by God. But God "exalted" Jesus, gave him the name above all names, Lord, and made every knee to bend, in acknowledgment of his lordship and acceptance of the new norms of the new community. Hope was given the oppressed that victory would follow humiliation and God's glory would ultimately prevail and transform the world.

VD

Prayer

Gentle God,

who in Jesus Christ

showed us humility and compassion,

we thank you for your gracious love.

Forgive our sin of pride and apathy,
empower us to struggle for justice,
for the sake of the most oppressed
and totally broken in body and spirit.

Compassionate Jesus,
teach us to be true disciples
in our times
in all places today.
Enable us to change attitudes and structures
that enslave.

Divine Wisdom, Holy Spirit,
in your grace, transform the world
in us, through us.
Cleanse our hearts, and renew our spirits.
With serving hands and liberating actions,
we humbly pray for courage and inspiration
to do your will, beginning today.

In Jesus' name, we hope and pray. Amen.

Elizabeth S. Tapia, 2005

Note:

1. Manu Dharma Shastra VIII 413-414 - a Sanskrit compendium of ancient laws and customs particularly revered in Brahminical Hinduism.

How to work with these texts

- Think about your community at home. Who would be most missed if they decided to withdraw their labour for a week? If you are in a group, ask everyone to think of their answer before going around to share responses. Compare the people on this list to those with the greatest social status in the community. How does this relate to the request of James and John in Mark 10:32-45 and Paul's description of Jesus in Philippians 2:1-11?

- Why do we commonly regard the role of a servant as being lowly and too often treat people who are servants accordingly? What difference should it make to us if we see Jesus as one who came to serve? How does your church describe those who are called to high office and leadership positions? Is this seen in terms of comfortable privilege or demanding responsibility? What does it mean for us, whether or not we hold an important position in the church, when we empty and humble ourselves, acting as servants or slaves, even to the extent of submission to ultimate self-sacrifice? How might the church and the world be changed if we did that?

- How does this Bible study help us understand and respond to the assembly theme "God, in your grace, transform the world"?

"My Grace Is Sufficient for You"

Isabel Apawo Phiri

Ezekiel 36:26-27

I will give you a new heart and put a new spirit in you; I will remove from you your heart of stone and give you a heart of flesh. And I will put my Spirit in you and move you to follow my decrees and be careful to keep my laws.

2 Corinthians 12:6-10

Even if I should choose to boast, I would not be a fool, because I would be speaking the truth. But I refrain, so no one will think more of me than is warranted by what I do or say. To keep me from becoming conceited because of these surpassingly great revelations there was given me a thorn in my flesh, a messenger of Satan, to torment me. Three times I pleaded with the Lord to take it away from me. But he said to me, "My grace is sufficient for you, for my power is made perfect in weakness." Therefore, I will boast all the more gladly about my weakness, so that Christ's power may rest in me. That is why, for Christ's sake, I delight in weaknesses, in insults, in hardships, in persecutions, in difficulties. For when I am weak, then I am strong.[1]

The passage from Ezekiel 36 is about God's relationship with the people of Israel. The people of Israel had been rebellious against God and were in exile at this time, where they experienced a lot of suffering. Through the prophet Ezekiel, God is the one who initiates change, taking away the heart of stubbornness in the people of Israel and putting in its place a transformed heart that is willing to work with God. In the Bible, flesh is used to mean weakness as opposed to strength. In this text it is used in comparison with hard stone, which is cold. God is promising to remove the coldness that was in the hearts of the people of Israel and to replace it with a teachable heart that is willing to do God's will. God will do this by bestowing God's spirit on the people.

Second Corinthians 12:6-10 comes as a fulfilment of Ezekiel's passage in Paul's life. Paul is talking about how God humbled him

Prof. Isabel Apawo Phiri is professor of African theology at the school of theology and religion, University of KwaZulu Natal, South Africa, and the coordinator of the Circle of Concerned African Women Theologians.

by putting a thorn in his flesh after he had deep spiritual experiences with God. Paul was empowered by these experiences, and they gave him more authority as an apostle of Christ. But God controlled Paul's power and authority so that Paul would perpetually depend on God's power. God guided Paul in regard to how to use this power. The thorn in Paul's flesh transformed Paul's use of spiritual power by forcing him to focus not on what he as a person was able to do but on what Christ could do through him despite the thorn in his flesh.

The main characters in the two passages

In the Ezekiel passage, the main character is God. We know that God is relational. In this passage we are reminded about God's covenant with the people of Israel, who are God's chosen nation.[2] God had a covenant with the people of Israel. This was an unequal relationship. God promised things to the people of Israel but defined conditions (Gen. 15; Ex. 20; Deut. 5:6-21). Throughout salvation history, God reminds the people of Israel about the special relationship they have. But on occasion, the people of Israel have disobeyed God's commands. The result was God allowing the people of Israel to be taken captive and experiencing life in exile, where they went through a very difficult time. God was now promising them restoration that would start with inner spiritual and moral transformation.

The main characters of 2 Corinthians 12:6-10 are Paul and God. Paul and God had a relationship (Acts 9). Paul did not meet the historical Jesus. In Acts 1:21-22 the qualifications of an apostle are given. According to this passage, Paul did not qualify to be an apostle of Christ. In previous passages of 2 Corinthians, Paul was accused of being a fool and weak, and it was argued that his apostleship was not genuine. Paul's apostolic authority and personal integrity were being questioned. His whole ministry was at stake. Therefore, Paul was pushed into a corner to defend himself and justify his apostleship. Paul was tempted to use his extraordinary spiritual experiences as justification for his superiority over other apostles. Instead, he decided to put the emphasis on his dependency on God's grace that had carried him through his ministry.

The thorn in Paul's flesh

New Testament scholars have debated the nature of Paul's thorn in his flesh, since Paul himself did not explain what it was. Some have suggested that it was a sickness that may have been one among the following: a speech defect, an eye problem or epilepsy. Others have suggested that it was a sensual temptation. Yet others have mentioned the constant persecutions that he went through. Whatever it was, God apparently did not see the need for us to know what it was, and speculation does not help us in any way. What is clear is that it was something that was brought about by an agent of Satan, under the permission of God, to control Paul's use of spiritual power. This can be linked to the experiences of Job, and of Jesus in the garden of Gethsemane. Paul and Jesus prayed that the problem that was facing them should be taken away. In both cases, God did not take the problem away because of God's own plans for humanity. Instead, God provided the grace to keep going in the midst of these problems.

When one reads this passage in the context of Africa, where there is untold suffering as a result of social injustices based on race, gender, class and ethnicity, one is tempted to mention the agents of Satan in Africa and ask God, "Why us, Lord?" However, neither mentioning Satan nor asking God "why?" solve the problem. What is spiritually disturbing is that God allows such suffering to exist even among deeply prayerful people. The central question is, why do people who put their faith in God suffer? The majority of African people are very spiritual. African churchwomen's organizations are known for their powerful prayers that are accompanied by fasting. It is not uncommon for one to hear mothers of Africa crying before God that the spirit of poverty, incurable diseases like HIV/AIDS, crime, unemployment, violence against women and children, and so on, should be bound and thrown into the lake of fire. Yet statistics show that the poor are getting poorer and the rich are getting richer. HIV/AIDS is still spreading unabated. Violence against women and children is increasing. The questions we need to ask ourselves are these: Are such problems spiritual, and can they be chased away only through prayer and fasting? Shouldn't we combine bold prayers with bold actions that come as a result of being empowered by the Spirit of God to seek the transformation of the structures that oppress us through the misuse of God-given power?

African Christians should not forget that we operate under God's grace as we live on earth. Africa is not the most sinful continent on earth nor is it most likely to attract God's wrath. For reasons that we will never fully understand, God allows injustice and inequalities, illnesses and diseases in our lives. We live in a fallen world that is groaning like a woman in childbirth. The causes of Africa's problems are both local and international. Sometimes prayers and actions remove the sources of suffering. At other times, prayer just serves to minimize the pain. Yet there are other times when "the messengers of Satan are not always overthrown here and now by prevailing prayer, though they will be overthrown ultimately".[3] What gives us the strength to go on struggling for the justice of God to be realized on earth is the resounding voice of God that says to us, "My grace is sufficient for you, for my power is made perfect in weakness."

Prayer

We thank you, Creator God,

for empowering each one of us with

your Holy Spirit to effect change.

We thank you because you will never leave us

or forsake us if we put our trust in you.

Even where there is suffering you are there and

you have a plan for your people.

Your plan is good and brings life in abundance,

even in the midst of suffering.

Thank you because you are a God of justice and

you want to see justice on earth.

Thank you for choosing us and working through us

to bring peace and justice where people are hurting.

Give us courage to do what we know is right,

and to trust you to take care of the things we cannot change.

Thank you for reminding us that your grace is sufficient

to see us through those things we cannot change.

In Jesus' name.

Amen.[4]

IAP

Notes:

1. These two passages are taken from *the New International Version Study Bible*.

2. The idea of being chosen by God sometimes leads to discrimination against other people who have also been created by God. God's people sometimes cause unnecessary suffering for those whom they do not consider God's people.

3. Paul Barnett, *The Message of 2 Corinthians*, Leicester, InterVasity Press, 1988, p.178.

4. By Isabel Apawo Phiri, adapted from her prayer in Musa Dube ed., *AfricaPraying: A Handbook on HIV/AIDS Sensitive Sermon Guidelines and Liturgy*, WCC Publications, 2003, p.129.

How to work with these texts

• "Why us, Lord?" Isabel Apawo Phiri points out the reasons why the people of Africa might cry out in that way. When have you felt that the burdens of pain and injustice have been too great to bear? Or that your faithfulness seems to count for nothing, and has not been rewarded by positive results? In a group, share your stories with one another. Be careful not to tell others what their story means for them. Instead use their stories to help you understand your own experience.

- Why, in Ezekiel 36, are the people described as having a heart of stone? Does this have any modern parallels in our experience? How does having a heart of stone, being stubborn and unfeeling, obstruct a relationship with God and the fulfilment of God's purposes for humanity? How does the Spirit renew us?

- In 2 Corinthians 12:10, Paul says that "when I am weak, then I am strong". Is this Paul's way of coming to terms with an uncomfortable reality, or is he proclaiming a significant truth? Think of some words that could be used to describe strength. How appropriate are each of them in the light of Paul's statement? What are we praying for when we pray for the church to be made strong? Think of examples of the church finding strength in weakness. How is God's grace sufficient for us?

- How does this Bible study help us understand and respond to the assembly theme "God, in your grace, transform the world"?

Water and the Well
Springing to Eternal Life

Serge Hackel

John 4:1-42

Now when Jesus learned that the Pharisees had heard, "Jesus is making and baptizing more disciples than John" – although it was not Jesus himself but his disciples who baptized – he left Judea and started back to Galilee.

But he had to go through Samaria. So he came to a Samaritan city called Sychar, near the plot of ground that Jacob had given to his son Joseph. Jacob's well was there, and Jesus, tired out by his journey, was sitting by the well. It was about noon. A Samaritan woman came to draw water, and Jesus said to her, "Give me a drink." (His disciples had gone to the city to buy food.) The Samaritan woman said to him, "How is it that you, a Jew, ask a drink of me, a woman of Samaria?" (Jews do not share things in common with Samaritans.) Jesus answered her, "If you knew the gift of God, and who it is that is saying to you, 'Give me a drink', you would have asked him, and he would have given you living water." The woman said to him, "Sir, you have no bucket, and the well is deep. Where do you get that living water? Are you greater than our ancestor Jacob, who gave us the well, and with his sons and his flocks drank from it?" Jesus said to her, "Everyone who drinks of this water will be thirsty again, but those who drink of the water that I will give them will never be thirsty. The water that I will give will become in them a spring of water gushing up to eternal life." The woman said to him, "Sir, give me this water, so that I may never be thirsty or have to keep coming here to draw water." Jesus said to her, "Go, call your husband, and come back." The woman answered him, "I have no husband." Jesus said to her, "You are right in saying, 'I have no husband'; for you have had five husbands, and the one you have now is not your husband. What you have said is true!" The woman said to him, "Sir, I see that you are a prophet. Our ancestors worshipped on this mountain, but you say that the place where people must worship is in Jerusalem." Jesus said to her, "Woman, believe me, the hour is coming when you will worship the Father neither on this mountain nor in Jerusalem. You

Archpriest Serge Hackel (d. 9 February 2005), of the Russian Orthodox Church, was editor of the journal Sobornost *for over thirty years. From 1984 he was in charge of the weekly religious broadcasts of the BBC Russian service. He was deeply involved in ecumenical work, and wrote extensively on Orthodox history and theology.*

worship what you do not know; we worship what we know, for salvation is from the Jews. But the hour is coming, and is now here, when the true worshippers will worship the Father in spirit and truth, for the Father seeks such as these to worship him. God is spirit, and those who worship him must worship in spirit and truth." The woman said to him, "I know that Messiah is coming (who is called Christ). When he comes, he will proclaim all things to us." Jesus said to her, "I am he, the one who is speaking to you."

Just then his disciples came. They were astonished that he was speaking with a woman, but no one said, "What do you want?" or, "Why are you speaking with her?" Then the woman left her water jar and went back to the city. She said to the people, "Come and see a man who told me everything I have ever done! He cannot be the Messiah, can he?" They left the city and were on their way to him. Meanwhile the disciples were urging him, "Rabbi, eat something." But he said to them, "I have food to eat that you do not know about." So the disciples said to one another, "Surely no one has brought him something to eat?" Jesus said to them, "My food is to do the will of him who sent me to complete his work. Do you not say, 'Four months more, then comes the harvest'? But I tell you, look around you, and see how the fields are ripe for harvesting. The reaper is already receiving wages and is gathering fruit for eternal life, so that sower and reaper may rejoice together. For here the saying holds true, 'One sows and another reaps.' I sent you to reap that for which you did not labour. Others have laboured, and you have entered into their labour." Many Samaritans from that city believed in him because of the woman's testimony, "He told me everything I have ever done." So when the Samaritans came to him, they asked him to stay with them; and he stayed there two days. And many more believed because of his word. They said to the woman, "It is no longer because of what you said that we believe, for we have heard for ourselves, and we know that this is truly the Saviour of the world."

Ezekiel 47:1-12

Then he brought me back to the entrance of the temple; there, water was flowing from below the threshold of the temple towards the east (for the temple faced east); and the water was flowing down from below the south end of the threshold of the temple, south of the altar. Then he brought me out by way of the north gate, and led me around on the outside to the outer gate that faces towards the east; and the water was coming out on the south side. Going on eastward with a cord in his hand, the man measured one thousand cubits, and then led me through the water; and it was ankle-deep. Again he measured one thousand, and led me through the water; and it was knee-deep. Again he measured one thousand, and led me through the water; and it was up to the waist. Again he measured one thousand, and it was a river that I could not cross, for the water had risen; it was deep enough to swim in, a river that could not be crossed. He said to me, "Mortal, have you seen this?"

Then he led me back along the bank of the river. As I came back, I saw on the bank of the river a great many trees on the one side and on the other. He said to me, "This water flows towards the eastern region and goes down into the Arabah; and when it enters the sea, the sea of stagnant waters, the water will become fresh. Wherever the river goes, every living creature that swarms will live, and there will be very many fish, once these waters reach there. It will become fresh; and everything will live where the river goes. People will stand fishing beside the sea from En-gedi to En-eglaim; it will be a place for the spreading of nets; its fish will be of a great many kinds, like the fish of the Great Sea. But its swamps and marshes will not become fresh; they are to be left for salt. On the banks, on both sides of the river, there will grow all kinds of trees for food. Their leaves will not wither nor their fruit fail, but they will bear fresh fruit every month, because the water for them flows from the sanctuary. Their fruit will be for food, and their leaves for healing."

Tiredness: Jesus pauses at the well of Sychar in his tiredness. That he is tired is an indication of his frailty, a reminder of his incarnation. He is for real.

But he is also more than merely real. As this gospel's prologue has established, he is none other than the Word made flesh. As such he dwells among us. So there is also a positive side to his tiredness. It is not only rooted in his incarnation, but ennobled by it. This in turn affects his fellow human beings. It allows for all their various kinds of tiredness to be rendered sacred.

Thirst: The same could be said of their thirst. Thirst is the prime concern of Jesus at the well. His request for a drink is supremely human. It is, moreover, universal. The human body is constructed to depend on water. The Saviour's request for a drink matches every individual's need. Moreover, it imbues this need with dignity.

But the "thirst" of this passage involves more than bodily needs. Tiredness may be a function and a burden of the daily round. Thirst has additional dimensions, as does the water which can quench it.

Living waters: So we are no longer merely in the realms of H_2O. There is talk of "living waters" that have an awesome power to well up to eternal life. This is not some modern commentator's fancy. "Living waters" were familiar to a prophet like Ezekiel. Here, the image provides the symbolism used by Jesus at this ancient well. The simple water of the well, as he points out, will always need to be replenished: the living waters which he offers in their stead will quench the drinker's inner thirst for ever.

Ezekiel's temple: Ezekiel in his time had visions of such waters pouring from the holiest source, the very heart of Israel. For streams of water issued from beneath the threshold of the temple, and they issued also from its sides. Plentiful and powerful as they were, the waters formed deep rivers, rivers which purified polluted waters and enriched them. They anticipated the crystal-clear waters of the New Jerusalem in the age to come. The book of Revelation was to see them flowing "from the throne of God and of the Lamb" (Rev. 22:1).

Holy places: But if Ezekiel had seen the temple in Jerusalem as the source from which such living waters flow, Samaritans could well respond with some dismay, "What about us?" For they rejected Jerusalem as a sacred centre. It is therefore not surprising that the woman at the well should juxtapose the rival holy places. Is the temple in Jerusalem the proper place to worship, together with the Jews? Or should one go to Mount Gerizim, in accordance with Samaritan tradition? This implied another question in respect of either: Should anybody's preference for the one mean condemnation of the other? For only one of them can be true, or so the woman must have thought.

Worship in spirit and in truth: Jesus is careful to express his preference for the worship in the Jerusalem temple since "salvation is from the Jews". But while he sees this as a welcome stepping-stone towards salvation, he straightaway goes further. For new perspectives are required. As it is, neither Samaritans nor Jews possess the wherewithal to worship as they should. It is not enough to have a holy place. Nor enough to be a holy nation. Over and above conventional, inherited religion, authentic worship calls for inspiration, and the readiness to be inspired. This alone ensures that worship is "in spirit and in truth".

Is this presented as a distant prospect, a challenge for the future? It could be, says Jesus, that the appropriate time has yet to come. Nevertheless, it is equally and simultaneously a challenge for the present. For the time is coming "and now is" (John 4:23). The paradox and sting is in that "and". It helps to introduce an urgent present, and with it comes a prompting to respond.

The role of the Spirit: Responding is not so easy, is the obvious reaction. Certainly not easy if we depend only on our limited resources. However, worship "in spirit and in truth" implies involvement of the Spirit, the one God, for "God is Spirit". So begins another of the Saviour's sayings at the well. No other force engenders, no other force empowers, worship in spirit and in truth. It is not as if the welling up of living waters speaks of something else. When John quotes other words of Jesus concerning the living waters flowing from his people, he does not hesitate to add, "by this he meant the Spirit" (John 7:37-39). No wonder the Orthodox so frequently invoke the Spirit with the words, "Come and abide in us."

Sacraments and symbols: In common with other Christians, and since early times, the Orthodox have sought to summon the image of living waters by means of sacraments and symbols. The symbols offer a façade which is not intended to exhaust the inner meaning of the sacramental act.

The waters of baptism are sanctified with an invocation of the Holy Spirit, that the Spirit may "indwell" us. So each and every member of the church emerges from the font covered with grace generated in those living and life-giving waters. In later years, the faithful may be offered blessed water to consume. Such water may also be sprinkled on their persons or their food. In the process, truths which remain beyond our rational comprehension may yet be tangibly expressed. They may be "marked, learned and inwardly digested".

Mission: Did the woman at the well heed and digest the exhortation to worship in spirit and in truth? She certainly abandoned her precious vessel then and there, so as to inform her neighbours of this visitor's potential for them all. She was obviously convinced that knowledge of his presence must be shared. Such was her missionary zeal. And the urgency with which she acts suggests some understanding of his answers.

Questions: But she is slow to recognize the limitations of her various questions. It is not that they are limited in scope. However, though they may have touched on sociology, topography, hydrology, archaeology and biblical tradition, they were simplistic in themselves. Were it not for her partner in the conversation, she hardly could have gained important insights from them, let alone illumination. Indeed, she could have proved a tiresome nuisance, and no more. Yet there he is, her partner, highlighting fruitful aspects of her questions, providing guidance in what has now become her search.

To be fair, she also makes some contributions of her own. The very persistence of her questions needs to be admired. Moreover, had there not been questions such as these, we might still lack the answers. Reticence on her part would have brought the woman from Samaria not much nearer to the truth, even though she might have acted in the "proper" fashion by accepting such degrees of social segregation as were practised in her day. Jesus, for his part, willingly accepts her questions, "outsider" though she be. Not only an outsider, but a woman. Jesus' disciples may have been perturbed by this, but not he.

Restricted water? Segregation had not prevented Jesus from requesting water at the well. If there was already talk of Samaritans as ritually unclean and with household vessels which no Jew should use, he was ready to ignore it. At a different level, and in a world where he himself encouraged people to worship in spirit and in truth, he could hardly impose restrictions on their use of living water, the water which was his. Later, in Jerusalem itself, and at the temple, he was firmly to extend his invitation to anyone who thirsts: "Let him come to me and drink."

Depleted resources: He was the channel for such living and life-giving water – in anticipation of the Spirit "which was not yet given". Even so, does there come a time when he finds himself depleted of such waters? Not that it is immediately apparent in the way it happened, since his needs are reflected in a simple exclamation from the cross, "I am thirsty" (John 19:28).

This could speak directly of his physical requirements at the time. Hence the reaction of his guards. And he himself is ready to accept their offer of a drink. Could the thirst be more profound than that, as well? Could it be the counterpart of yet another exclamation, or quotation, from the cross, "My God, my God, why have you forsaken me?" Here is one of the most anguished moments of the incarnation: Jesus ponders his own vocation as the Son of God. His thirst would seem to contradict the teachings at the well. But he has plumbed the very depths of anguish, and so has overcome it.

Superabundant grace: When the book of Revelation touches on the prospect of the age to come, it shows the New Jerusalem to be a place where any thirst is likely to be quenched. So "let the thirsty come", urges the narrator in this section of the book: "Let whoever wishes accept the water of life as a gift" (Rev. 21:6, 22:17).

On the earthly plane, newcomers to church life may have received their call to be baptized in words like these. But the message has wider implications. Superabundant grace is freely made available to all.

An acclamation from the Orthodox service of matins for the theophany of our Lord

O King without beginning, through the communion of the Spirit,

Thou dost anoint and make perfect the nature of mankind.

Thou hast cleansed us in the undefiled streams,

putting to shame the arrogant force of darkness,

and now Thou dost translate it unto endless life.[1]

Note:

1. From *The Festal Menaion*, translated Mother Mary and Archimandrite Kallistos Ware, London, Faber & Faber, 1969, pp.381-82.

How to work with these texts

• Water is a universal human need, as Serge Hackel reminds us. In some situations, thirst is a life-threatening daily reality, in others we may use thirst as a metaphor for deep needs and desires. What do people thirst for in your local community? Who and what satisfies that thirst? Be specific and realistic. Where does the living and life-bringing water of John 4 and Ezekiel 47 fit into this?

• In what ways did Jesus challenge traditional assumptions about relationships and about worship in John 4? What is the significance of the conversation for the Samaritan woman and her community? What can we learn from that?

- How do we use water sacramentally, symbolically and metaphorically in the worship and life of the churches? Recognize the differences between traditions.

- Serge Hackel suggests, "It is not enough to have a holy place. Nor enough to be a holy nation. Over and above conventional, inherited religion, authentic worship calls for inspiration, and the readiness to be inspired." How do we open ourselves to the inspiration of the Spirit so that our worship is experienced as worship in spirit and in truth?

- The vision in Ezekiel 47 is of life-bringing water flowing from the place where God is worshipped. What flows out into the world from our worship? How can the living water given by Jesus bring new life to our worship, and thus to the world?

- How does this Bible study help us understand and respond to the assembly theme "God, in your grace, transform the world"?

"In God's Word I Hope"

Meloyan Vaghinag

Relationship in the interaction of God.

Psalm 130

Out of the depths I cry to you, O Lord. Lord, hear my voice! Let your ears be attentive to the voice of my supplications! If you, O Lord, should mark iniquities, Lord, who could stand? But there is forgiveness with you, so that you may be revered. I wait for the Lord, my soul waits, and in his word I hope; my soul waits for the Lord more than those who watch for the morning, more than those who watch for the morning. O Israel, hope in the Lord! For with the Lord there is steadfast love, and with him is great power to redeem. It is he who will redeem Israel from all its iniquities.

2 Corinthians 3:18

And all of us, with unveiled faces, seeing the glory of the Lord as though reflected in a mirror, are being transformed into the same image from one degree of glory to another; for this comes from the Lord, the Spirit.

Psalm 130 is the outburst of an afflicted spirit: "Out of the depths." Obviously the psalmist is in serious distress, but we do not know exactly in what kind of distress he is. Probably his life is threatened and he is attacked by the enemy, or he is undergoing some inward spiritual crisis. Whatever the circumstances are, one thing is very clear: that the psalmist is not swallowed up by the distress surrounding him, but persists in believing and hoping in God.

The spirit of hope in his soul is much greater than the spirit of hopelessness. For him, distresses are not opportunities to murmur and grumble against God; rather, they are opportunities to look up to heaven and ask for God's intervention. He does not focus his attention on the difficulties lying in his path but on God who is able to remove all kinds of difficulties. He has a believing spirit. He prays, and he is confident that God's delivering grace will follow his prayer.

Father Meloyan Vaghinag, who was ordained in 1995, is a member of the brotherhood of the Catholicosate of Cilicia, Lebanon. After graduating from the seminary of the Catholicosate, he studied for two years at Pittsburgh Theological Seminary in the USA. He is currently the director of the Bible studies/theological education department of the Catholicosate of Cilicia, Armenian Apostolic Church.

When he thinks of his iniquities, he is filled with fear lest the Lord should mark his sins. "If you, O Lord, should mark iniquities, Lord, who could stand?" (v.3). He knows that if God demands an accounting of his iniquities, there can be no hope for him. But he is confident that God would not do so, because God is the kind of God who casts all his sins behind his back (Isa. 38:17). The psalmist is sure that God is not interested in his sins, but in him. He knows that God does not count his transgressions and wrongdoings, but he takes full account of him.

The psalmist pictures himself as someone who needs forgiveness, mercy and redemption, and God as someone who has all those things (vv.4,7). The psalmist is asking for God's forgiveness, by which he indicates that he has a real conviction of his own sins. This leads him to cry to God "out of the depths"; out of the depths of unfaithfulness, of disobedience, of transgressions. No one can cry "out of the depths" unless he or she feels the destructive power of sin within himself or herself.

Verses 5 and 6 show that the author has absolute faith in God's forgiveness: "I wait for the Lord, my soul waits, and in his word I hope; my soul waits for the Lord more than those who watch for the morning." The psalmist waited and received God's blessings. Anyone who does not know how to wait does not receive God's blessings. "In God's word I hope." The word of God is the hope of the hopeless ones. There is a delivering power in God's word, a life-giving strength. "Lord, to whom can we go? You have the word of eternal life" (John 6:68). To put our hope in the word of God means to rise out of the "depths". No one ever hoped and then remained in the "depths". God is a restoring God.

Verses 7 and 8 tell us that the psalmist got what he asked for. Now he is out of the depths in which he at first found himself, and so he can encourage and exhort the people of Israel to put their hope in the Lord. He testifies that "with the Lord there is steadfast love, and with him is great power to redeem". He would not exhort others to put their hope in the Lord if he had been disappointed himself. He has no doubt that the God who redeemed him will also redeem the Israelites. He knows for sure that the Lord will not fail the people, just as God did not fail him personally.

Verse 8 does not speak about the deliverance of the people of Israel, but about their redemption. Redemption needs sacrifice. The Son of God became that sacrifice. His sacrificial death emancipated not only the Israelites but the entire world from eternal death.

The psalmist testifies that God not only has redeemed him from his iniquities, and not only has removed his penalty, but also has granted him peace, joy and new life. This inner joy is the result of forgiveness. No one can have this inner joy and peace if he or she is not forgiven.

"And all of us, with unveiled faces, seeing the glory of the Lord as though reflected in a mirror, are being transformed into the same image from one degree of glory to another; for this comes from the Spirit of the Lord" (2 Cor. 3:18). In verse 16 the apostle Paul speaks about the vital importance of turning to Christ in order for the veil to be removed. In verse 17 he talks about the real freedom which is the result of receiving the Holy Spirit. No one can receive the Holy Spirit unless he or she turns to Christ. Turning to Christ and receiving the Holy Spirit will enable us to reflect the glory of the Lord. To reflect the glory of the Lord means to go through gradual spiritual transfiguration. There can be no spiritual transfiguration without the transforming power of the Holy Spirit. Christ's Spirit helps us to grow in the glory of Christ. The Holy Spirit is the one who restores in us the image and the likeness of Christ.

Paul knows by his own experience that the veil will be removed from the life of those who become Christians, and they will go "from glory to glory", "from strength to strength" (Ps. 84:7), and he wants everybody to come to that knowledge. By the words "from glory to glory", of course, Paul does not refer to worldly splendour, but to spiritual excellence and perfection.

Without faith there can be no gradual process of spiritual assimilation. Using the faith granted to us by God leads us to perfection. To have faith in Christ grants us the power which produces assimilation into Christ. Faith justifies us. Faith sanctifies us. Faith changes us. When we use the word "change" we do not mean merely a change of feeling, or opinion, or even behaviour, but a change of *being*.

Our heavenly Father changes us into the divine likeness, a likeness that we lost through the fall. By the constant work of the Holy Spirit in our hearts, we become like Christ. And when we become like Christ, we reflect the glory and beauty of the Father, because Christ "is the reflection of the Father's glory and the exact imprint of the Father's very being" (Heb. 1:3).

What does it mean to be assimilated into Christ? Or what should we do in order to be assimilated into Christ? First, we have to ask Christ to become "the pioneer and perfecter of our faith" (Heb. 12:2), and second, we have to invite him to live his own life in our lives. By doing so, he will renew us in his own image by the gracious presence and work of the Holy Spirit.

No one can apprehend the transforming power of a pure Christianity without this doctrine of spiritual operation. Going through such spiritual operation will make us not only kind and good Christians, but also Christians who are reformed and born again. In other words, kind and good people are not the ones who can be assimilated into Christ, but reformed and born-again people are the ones who can be so.

Christians who claim that they have been born again and renewed must not live a life different from the life of Christ. They shall not only bear the name of Christ, but also the character and characteristics of Christ, the identity and the individuality of Christ, the personality and the distinctiveness of Christ. Hence, to be assimilated into Christ means to have the forgiving spirit of Christ, the loving heart of Christ, the prayerful mind of Christ and, along with all these, to become the restoring and regenerating presence of Christ in the life of lost humanity.

Accepting Christ as the door of salvation will enable us to lead others to salvation. In this way, we are truly assimilated into Christ.

MV

Prayer

God of unity, God of love,

what we say with our lips, make strong in our hearts.

What we affirm with our minds, make vivid in our lives.

Send us your Spirit

to pray in us what we dare not pray,

to claim us beyond our own claims,

to bind us when we are tempted to go our own ways.

Lead us forward.

Lead us together.

Lead us to do your will,

the will of Jesus Christ, our Lord. Amen.[1]

Note:

1. *Together on the Way,* WCC Publications, 1999, pp.115-16.

How to work with these texts

• Why is asking for and receiving forgiveness important for good relationships between individuals, communities and nations? What does offering forgiveness and being forgiven do for "victims" and "offenders"? What is the significance of our requests for forgiveness in the Lord's prayer and in our liturgies? In what ways can we identify with the writer of Psalm 130?

- Meloyan Vaghinag reminds us that the writer is severely afflicted but not in hopeless despair. Read Psalm 130 verse by verse and identify the phrases which indicate the writer's faith and trust in God. What do these tell us about the writer, and about God?

- Does this psalm imply that God will rescue us from affliction and restore the status quo, or does the idea of forgiveness mean that we are forever changed? How have we experienced God's response to our cries out of the depths?

- Read 2 Corinthians 3:18. What does it mean to be transformed, through the work of Christ and the Holy Spirit, "from one degree of glory to another"?

- How does this Bible study help us understand and respond to the assembly theme "God, in your grace, transform the world"?

That Grace May Abound

Concluding Reflections from Latin America

Israel Batista

"Grace, the cross and hope" is the topic for a continent-wide community study in Latin America. It raises a challenge to reflect on grace in the midst of a world that has been tainted by "disgrace". There are so many who are poor, there is such a need for justice on earth. The realities of suffering, pain and desperation, affecting the lives of our people, are knocking at our door. Can we really talk of God's grace when we are affected by such penury?

Listening to our churches and taking the pulse of Latin America, we, theologians and biblical scholars from different denominations and with different theological view-points, have become convinced that our people seek an understanding of the grace of God, are longing for the merciful, loving attitude of God, as father and mother, open to all God's children and inviting us to have a life full of trust and hope.

There are not many terms that are equally as central to biblical thought as is the word "grace". Following St Augustine and the 16th-century reformers, the Swiss theologian Karl Barth emphasized the importance of the relationship between grace and gratitude (*charis/eucharistia*) by insisting that grace should be the central principle of our theology and gratitude the driving force of our ethics. The Heidelberg Catechism affirms that we need to know three truths: how great our sins and misery are, how great God's grace is in delivering us, and how grateful we are to be for God's grace.

Everything, from creation (Gen. 1:31), through the building of a nation with a mission to bless all nations, culminating in the incarnation of the Son of God (John 1:14) is clear evidence of God's grace, generosity and favour towards the whole of creation (Ps. 104).

The Bible does not ignore the magnitude of human sin, and the cross that demonstrates the tragedy does not allow for any false

Rev. Israel Batista, from Cuba, is general secretary of the Latin American Council of Churches (CLAI). He writes on behalf of the Latin American theological commission.

optimism. This dark reality, which led to the rise of a whole sacrificial and priestly system, is confronted with the gratuity of God's action. In the words of the apostle Paul, "… where sin increased, grace abounded all the more" (Rom. 5:20).

At the beginning of his ministry, Jesus aligned himself with the prophetic tradition of announcing the jubilee, freedom and the year of the Lord's favour (Luke 4:18-21). Forgiveness, abundant life, the new beginning of human history were all there in the life and ministry of Jesus. His love for the poor, the sick, children, sinners, prostitutes and the lonely was an integral part of his proclamation in Nazareth. God's divine, free grace with new life in Christ responds to a history of human rebellion against God. Jesus does not require merit in those he calls; on the contrary, it is to those who are "weary and carrying heavy burdens" that he promises rest and health. His own death on the cross, the supreme manifestation of sin – human, individual and structural – is transformed by the grace of God into a reaffirmation of his saving mission in and through the ultimate sacrifice.

The apostle Paul discovered the meaning of God's freely given grace through his experience on the road to Damascus. He felt accepted through no merit of his own. In the letter to Philemon, in which the runaway slave is returned to his master, Philemon is encouraged to receive him as a brother. There is no longer a relationship of purchase and property, no longer an obligation by law or through force: there is an acceptance of brotherhood, of fraternity, of the new reality that God has brought in Jesus Christ.

In today's world, there is a growing sense that everything is a commodity, that everything has a price, that there is no such thing as a free lunch; the overall culture, which keeps us all captive, is based on one distinction: whether we produce or we consume. It is important to go back to Paul's idea that everything is free in God's relationship with the nations, that everything is love in God's relationship with creation.

The Latin American theological commission (CTL), which comes together under the auspices of the Latin American Council of Churches (CLAI), has in recent years articulated its thinking on the topic "Grace, the cross and hope" in the following points:

- God's grace and love, freely given, are the way into Christian life. The understanding of the unconditional availability of God, who accepts us as we are, affects our relationship with the culture around us and the whole ecosystem: nothing is outside the purpose of God's love. Nothing can be outside the realm of those who feel part of that resolve. We are free so that we can free others; we are loved so that we can love others.

- To experience grace is to experience rest and repose in God. The church is called to celebrate God's good provision. This is why celebration is part of its daily life. Celebration expresses the irrepressible joy of those who know that, no matter what happens in the world, God has the last word. The affection, the fraternal support, of those in the faith community is a sign of the movement of the love of God as we are accepted and rehabilitated. Celebration and praise correspond to the knowledge that God's love is freely given to each one of us. Churches are therefore not communities of law or discipline, but rather communities of celebration, rejoicing, joy and hope.

- In our region and in the world, the force of the economic system that marginalizes large sectors is anti-grace, is dis-grace. Faced with a dehumanizing market, political schemes with no credibility, a judicial system that favours the powerful, systemic corruption, a loss of values breaking up our families, communities and societies..., "God is able to provide you with every blessing in abundance" (2 Cor. 9:8). God's gift of grace means that the hope of life is poured out through the cross. Grace, in a Latin American context, means dealing with the realities of life, the cross, yet with a sense of hope. Grace is God's gift in the face of a loss of hope. Our churches are communities of the Spirit, where we have learned to live God's grace in Christ.

    It is not easy to act as God wants, to live in accordance with kingdom values. It seems that grace is seen in two extremes today: either experienced as whimsical moods, limited to private feelings, or recited as a definitive catechism, with a concern for orthodoxy. Neither of these extremes is faithful to the spirit of the gospel. In today's society every man and woman has to fight to "be somebody", to be worthy. This logic is so different and contrary to that of grace! In exclusive societies, recognition of human dignity is selective.

- It is important to link grace and human dignity; both refer to God, and both refer to the human being. Human dignity and divine grace are inseparable because it is not possible to experience God's grace without human dignity. Where there is no human dignity, there is an absence of God's grace; where there is human dignity, in some way God's grace and God's glory are present.

We feel that God's grace, as a blessing from on high, is walking around our streets and cities, running through our fields and towns, knocking on the doors of our homes and communities, reaching into our lives and renewing our motivation and spirituality. We can say without doubt that we are living in the "*kairos* of grace": may grace abound.

Appendix
Rationale for the Choice of Texts

Luke 4:16-30 • Isaiah 61:1-4

The proclamation of the "year of the Lord" is God's answer to the prayer of the assembly theme. Luke 4 is Jesus' (or the Spirit's) manifesto, setting the priorities for Christ's ministry and the church's mission, and has particular resonance in Latin America. Jesus' sermon links pneumatology with transforming justice, good news to the poor, healing and liberation. Jesus preaches that Isaiah 61 is valid from now on, at any time and for all time, and it includes all people. That last point created a major conflict between Jesus and the people, especially the leaders of that time, foreshadowing the cross.

Isaiah 65:17-25 • Revelation 21:1-8

God's creative and transforming power makes all things new, now and in the future. The focus of Isaiah 65 is on justice, peace and life in abundance as a realistic and medium-term hope, expressed in socio-economic and political terms, while also pointing to a reality beyond the horizons of history. Revelation 21 extends the hope to a coming fullness of communion with God, overcoming even death, without however neglecting to link God's free gift to ethical challenges for a transformation of individual lives.

Jonah 4:1-11 • Acts 10:9-35

The book of Jonah is a story about the transformation of a "foreign people" (near today's Baghdad) and even of God, whose grace surpasses all understanding, in particular the understanding of Jonah himself and that of "God's people". Consequently the passage challenges our understanding of and approach to people of other cultures and religions. Acts 10 echoes Jonah: Peter's transformation not only changes his attitude, but will make him instrumental in modifying the church's mission. Both texts show how, through encounters with others and with God, the fundamentals of our faith may be questioned.

Philippians 2:1-11 • Mark 10:32-45

The hymn of Philippians 2 celebrates the incarnation as Christ's kenosis (or self-emptying) and identification with suffering humanity, with the humble and humiliated. The message of cross and resurrection is at the centre of the New Testament message of God's grace and the centre also of the transformation this implies for traditional views about God and God's messengers. Philippians 2 also calls for a change in the disciples' life-style and in relationships within the community of the church (v.4: "let the same mind be in you that was in Christ Jesus"). Other conclusions from Christ's self-emptying approach appear in the parallel text from Mark's gospel, which contains a fundamental critique of the use of power by political authorities and a challenge to the church to consider an alternative use of power as one of its essential marks (v.43: "it is not so among you").

2 Corinthians 12:6-10 • Ezekiel 36:26-27

We wanted to include one of the major Pauline texts on grace, without however falling into the denominational debate on "grace and law". Second Corinthians 12 links the experience of God's grace and empowerment with human vulnerability which can refer here both to persecution (or martyrdom) and to illness. Grace does not eliminate suffering, but transforms it. The text is central also for a link between the assembly theme and the Decade to Overcome Violence's focus on the use, abuse and misuse of power. Second Corinthians can be read as a fulfilment of the promise of God's Spirit announced in Ezekiel 37, with an emphasis on costly grace. In the Latin American context, 2 Corinthians is an important antidote to the theology of prosperity.

John 4:1-42 • Ezekiel 47:1-12

New insights may be drawn from the dialogue between Jesus and the Samaritan woman when it is read in relation to the assembly theme. Jesus announces and embodies God's gift of grace through his attitude to and dialogue with the woman. This leads to a transformation of her life, but also of the life of the community of that Samaritan town. It also presents quite a challenge to his disciples. Jesus' message also implies a change in the understanding of what is meant by worshipping God. Ezekiel's extraordinary vision of the water flowing from God's temple has similarities with John 4.

The water has transforming and healing power, and brings life in fullness.

Psalm 130 • 2 Corinthians 3:18

Psalm 130 is traditionally referred to as *de profundis*. It is a prayer of desperation and of hope, out of an extreme situation of social, economic or personal suffering, and it counts on God's forgiveness and grace. It offers a parallel to the assembly theme and raises questions about our understanding of God, our expectations of God and the link with our own commitment and engagement. Second Corinthians 3:18 is a classical text on transformation, or more precisely transfiguration (metamorphosis), and can appear as the challenging response to the prayer of the psalm. The freedom given by the Spirit, which illuminates communion with God, continually transforms human lives as they grow towards perfection.

Notes

60

Notes